Wildflowers of North America

a postcard collection by the National Wildflower Research Center

From wetlands to deserts, mountains to valleys, forests to prairies, the diversity of our North American wildflowers creates a patchwork of color and character across the continent. Tiny alpine plants of the tundra zone, cacti and succulents of arid regions, orchids of bogs and forests—all give testament to the genetic fine-tuning of time. Each region has a combination of both specialized wildflowers that grow only under a combination of certain conditions, and those that seem to thrive almost anywhere.

Whether growing in solitude or covering acres, each wildflower tells a story of connection —with local climate and soils, with plants nearby, with animals and insects that share the land. Those who follow, photograph, or study wildflowers begin to recognize some of those connections. Yet to know a wildflower is more than learning its scientific name or medicinal uses. Wildflowers call to our spirits, remind us of nature's cycles, and invite us to participate in their seasonal celebrations.

This postcard collection from the National Wildflower Research Center features examples of our diverse heritage of native wildflowers—a visual call to the w

Published by Voyageur Press

Printed in Hong Kong
92 93 94 95 96 5 4 3 2 1

ISBN 0-89658-202-7

Published by
VOYAGEUR PRESS, INC.
P.O. Box 338, 123 North Second Street
Stillwater, MN 55082 U.S.A.
From Minnesota and Canada 612-430-2210
Toll-free 800-888-9653

Voyageur Press books are also available at discounts for quantities for educational, fundraising, premium, or sales-promotion use. For details contact the marketing department.
Please write or call for our free catalog of publications and our free newsletter, *Wingbeat*.

Join the National Wildflower Research Center and help make a positive change in our environment!

The loss of native flora has fragmented and significantly altered natural environments across North America and other continents. Created in 1982 by Lady Bird Johnson, the Wildflower Center encourages the propagation and cultivation of North America's native plants and wildflowers for use in planned landscapes. The conservation and reestablishment of native plants restores lost wildlife habitat, conserves and protects the quality of water supplies, prevents topsoil erosion, and preserves biodiversity, all of which are essential to the health of the planet.

You can help further the Wildflower Center's educational programs, as well as our scientific research into the cultivation and propagation of native plants—helping heal the earth, by becoming a member of the Wildflower Center. A $25 membership will bring you the following benefits (and more!):

❖ A subscription to the Wildflower Center's information-packed newsletter and journal.
❖ Free native plant fact sheets and information from our botanists.
❖ Reciprocal privileges at more than 80 botanic gardens.
❖ Discounts on purchases of Wildflower Center merchandise.

Won't you join us as a member?

(complete the reverse side of this card)

National **W**ildflower **R**esearch **C**enter
2600 FM 973 North
Austin, Texas 78725-4201
(512) 929-3600

FROM: *(fill in your name, address, and phone)*

Name_____

Address_____

City_____

State, Zip_____

Phone_____

❒ Enclosed is my check for $25 *(enclose this card in an envelope)*.
❒ Please send me more information about the Wildflower Center.

MAIL TO:

National **W**ildflower **R**esearch **C**enter
2600 FM 973 North
Austin, Texas 78725-4201

Often blooming before snowmelt, **pasque flower** (*Anemone patens*) is one of the earliest spring wildflowers of prairies and mountains. Pasque flower is the state flower of South Dakota.

Found in alpine zones of the northern Rockies, **Jones' columbine** (*Aquilegia jonesii*) grows on rocky slopes and crevices. It was named after Marcus E. Jones, a botanist who studied Great Basin flora in the late 1800s.

A **columbine** of the Great Basin, *Aquilegia scopulorum* grows on limestone cliffs at high altitudes. Columbines are members of the buttercup family.

check with post office for postage

Prickly poppies (*Argemone* spp.) grow in dry, rocky soils of plains and hillsides. Native Americans have used plants in this genus to treat cataracts and other ailments.

From Wildflowers of North America, *a postcard collection.* © *by the National Wildflower Research Center. Published by Voyageur Press, 123 N. 2nd St., Stillwater, MN 55082 U.S.A. 612-430-2210; toll-free 800-888-9653.*

check with post office for postage
❖

Lush and inviting displays of native wildflowers attract a variety of butterflies, moths, and other insects.

check with post office for postage

The fragile beauty of **sego lily** (*Calochortus nuttallii*) softens harsh desert landscapes. The species name honors Thomas Nuttall, a plant collector of the early 1800s.

check with post office for postage

Trumpet honeysuckle (*Lonicera sempervirens*) occurs in woods and thickets throughout the eastern United States. The tubular red flowers attract hummingbirds.

© *by Julia Sanders. From* Wildflowers of North America, *a postcard collection by the National Wildflower Research Center Published by Voyageur Press, 123 N. 2nd St., Stillwater, MN 55082 U.S.A. 612-430-2210; toll-free 800-888-9653.*

Rosita (*Centaurium calycosum*) grows in open areas of the Southwest. According to Greek mythology, the centaur used plants in this genus to heal wounds.

The translucent flowers of **beach morning glory** (*Convolvulus soldanella*) are a familiar sight along Pacific coasts. The plant's long runners help stabilize coastal sand dunes.

check with post office for postage
❖

As its name suggests, **showy lady's slipper** (*Cypripedium reginae*) is one of the most striking orchids of the Northeast. It is especially common in moist woods around the Great Lakes.

© *by W. D. Bransford. From* Wildflowers of North America, *a postcard collection by the National Wildflower Research Center. Published by Voyageur Press, 123 N. 2nd St., Stillwater, MN 55082 U.S.A. 612-430-2210; toll-free 800-888-9653.*

This dwarf **wallflower** (*Erysimum amoenum*) grows high in the alpine zones of the Rocky Mountains. Its rose-colored petals set this species apart from the more common yellow ones.

© *by W. D. Bransford. From* Wildflowers of North America, *a postcard collection by the National Wildflower Research Center. Published by Voyageur Press, 123 N. 2nd St., Stillwater, MN 55082 U.S.A. 612-430-2210; toll-free 800-888-9653.*

The orange-gold of **California poppy** (*Eschscholzia californica*) often turns entire hillsides aglow in the spring. In keeping with the "golden state," the poppy is California's state flower.

© *by W. D. Bransford. From* Wildflowers of North America, *a postcard collection by the National Wildflower Research Center. Published by Voyageur Press, 123 N. 2nd St., Stillwater, MN 55082 U.S.A. 612-430-2210; toll-free 800-888-9653.*

Often confused with asters, **fleabanes** (*Erigeron* spp.) bloom throughout North America in open, disturbed areas. Teas made from the dried leaves have been used to treat sore throats.

check with post office for postage
❖

Also called firewheel, **Indian blanket** (*Gaillardia pulchella*) grows in prairies and along roadsides. It is the state flower of Oklahoma.

Bottle gentian (*Gentiana andrewsii*) grows in moist woods and thickets throughout eastern North America. Also called closed gentian, the flowers never open fully.

© *by W. D. Bransford. From* Wildflowers of North America, *a postcard collection by the National Wildflower Research Center. Published by Voyageur Press, 123 N. 2nd St., Stillwater, MN 55082 U.S.A. 612-430-2210; toll-free 800-888-9653.*

Ajo-lily (*Hesperocallis undulata*) often seems out of place in dunes and gravel flats of the Southwest. The edible bulb is similar to garlic, *ajo* in Spanish.

Easy to recognize with its "puff ball" flowers and trailing form, **sensitive briar** (*Schrankia uncinata*) grows in sandy soils of prairies and open areas. The leaves curl up when touched.

Widespread throughout warm-temperate and tropical regions, **morning glories** thrive in open, disturbed areas. The blue flowers of this species (*Ipomoea hederacea*) turn purple with age.

check with post office for postage ❖

Desert four o'clock (*Mirabilis multiflora*) grows in sandy soils of pinon-juniper woodlands, deserts, and grasslands. The flowers open late in the afternoon.

Showy orchis (*Orchis spectabilis*) occurs in damp woods of eastern North America. The flower's long spur is filled with sweet nectar.

check with post office for postage
❖

Often found in exposed, calcareous soils, **Missouri prim-rose** (*Oenothera macrocarpa*) grows in prairies and along rocky hillsides and cliffs.

check with post office for postage
❖

Phlox species occur throughout North America in various forms—including cushiony mounds in alpine zones, tall perennials in the East, and low-growing annuals in the South.

check with post office for postage
❖

Well adapted to dry climates, **cut-leaf penstemon** (*Penstemon baccharifolius*) grows on limestone ledges and bluffs in West Texas. The waxy leaves help prevent water loss.

Stokes' aster (*Stokesia laevis*) occurs in coast plain pineland from northern Florida to Louisiana. It was named after Jonathon Stokes, an English physician.

© *by Julia Sanders. From* Wildflowers of North America, *a postcard collection by the National Wildflower Research Center. Published by Voyageur Press, 123 N. 2nd St., Stillwater, MN 55082 U.S.A. 612-430-2210; toll-free 800-888-9653.*

The colorful "pitchers" of the **crimson pitcher plant** (*Sarracenia leucophylla*) are deadly to insects that fall into the pitchers' standing water. Also known as the **fiddler's trumpet,** this flower occurs in bogs in the southeastern states.

check with post office for postage ❖

Trilliums are treats for forest hikers in the springtime. This **large-flowered trillium** (*Trillium grandiflorum*) occurs from Ontario and Quebec south to Georgia.

check with post office for postage ❖

Many species of **paintbrush** grow abundantly throughout the West. This species (*Castilleja parviflora*) is found in mountain meadows of the Northwest at moderate altitudes.

check with post office for postage
❖

The **white-rayed mule's ears** (*Wyethia helianthoides*), a member of the sunflower family, carpets valleys in many western states.

© *by W. D. Bransford. From* Wildflowers of North America, *a postcard collection by the National Wildflower Research Center. Published by Voyageur Press, 123 N. 2nd St., Stillwater, MN 55082 U.S.A. 612-430-2210; toll-free 800-888-9653.*

The wildflowers of each region give nature lovers a glimpse of the great diversity of our native flora.

check with post office for postage

Common milkweed (*Asclepias syriaca*) grows widespread throughout eastern North America. Like other milkweeds, it provides food for monarch butterflies and their larvae.

check with post office for postage
❖